Cooking For Two

81 Delicious And Healthy Recipes Perfectly Portioned To Serve Two Persons

MARINA BEECHER

ISBN-13:978-1973702153

ISBN-10:1973702150

DEDICATION

For Wilma! For all the years we ate together!

TABLE OF CONTENTS

INTRODUCTION

Cooking is a delight! Cooking for two is even more delightful. As small family units, young couples and "roomies" increase by the day, cooking for two becomes a necessity. Eating in a restaurant or ordering takeout is far more expensive and does not have the fresh taste of home cooking. Cooking at home for two also helps reduce waste and add more value per spending.

Each recipe in this book has been grouped into different segments: breakfasts, appetizers and snacks, salads, soups, desserts and drinks, main dishes- chicken, seafood and beef. This helps you to express your power of choice and guides you to make calculated meal decisions per time.

The unique taste of each recipe has a surprising way of making close relationships even more special. I guarantee that you will love every recipe you try out. Despite the great taste of each recipe, they are quite low in calorie and therefore you can be sure of nutritious and great tasting meals that will keep you fit.

One striking thing about this book is that it has a variety of recipes that are easy and quick to prepare, with ingredients that are easily available. The book makes even an amateur feel like a Pro!

Getting Everything Set For Cooking

Convenient cooking starts when you have all what you'll need for cooking a great meal. From the cooking equipments to the least of all ingredients, you need to get your kitchen and pantry thoroughly furnished with the necessities of everyday cooking. Imagine starting out to make a pancake or omelet for breakfast and suddenly realizing that there are no eggs or how would your soup taste without salt and pepper? It is very important to keep an ingredient list and note when any item is getting exhausted. This will help you in making your grocery shopping list.

Items You Need To Include In Your Grocery List.

Here are a couple of things you should always include in your grocery shopping list.

A carton of eggs: You'll need eggs in most breakfast recipes, snack recipes, sides and even some main dishes. You wouldn't want to miss those eggs on the store shelf.

Carbs: One or two packs each of pasta should take you through a whole week.

Fruits: A box of strawberries, a bunch of bananas, some apples, grapes, avocados, lemon and lime.

Vegetables: Eggplants, tomatoes, mushrooms, carrots, garlic, onions, potatoes, cilantro, parsley and some greens.

Breads: It is preferable to get fresh bread from the bakery. Get some sliced bread for sandwiches, buns for burgers and some dinner rolls.

Protein: stock up on salmon strips, fish filets, chicken breasts, frozen shrimps and steaks. Don't forget to add one or two cans of ground beef and turkey.

Cheese: Get some shredded cheese which great with quesadillas and pasta e.g. Mexican cheese blend and parmesan. The hard cheese goes well on snacks lick crackers so you definitely would not want to leave out your cheddar and Monterey Jack cheeses.

Milk and yogurt

Other must haves with longer shelf life: Olive oil, balsamic vinegar, salt, dry pepper, soy sauce etc.

Some Tools And Equipments For Small Scale Cooking

- Small saucepans: get saucepans with fitted lids ranging from ¾-1 quart for rice and starchy vegetable and 2-3 quart saucepans for probably your soups and steaming vegetables.
- Mini food processor/blender: for your couple-sized soups, pesto and sauces.
- Toaster broiler pan (oven size): The pan together with the rack can be used for broiling fish or garlic bread and for resting and salting steaks. The roasting pan can be used alone to roast vegetables or bake biscuits.
- Small ceramic or glass baking dishes: great vessels for marinating, breading before frying and baking casseroles.
- A large/medium mesh strainer: use this instead of a bulky colander.
- A set of measuring spoons, cups and mixing bowls
- An 8-inch cast iron skillet: very indispensable; you can't set up a kitchen without a skillet or a frying pan.
- Wooden/heat resistant plastic spatula and spoons, a metal slotted spoon and a wire whisk.
- A knife set which includes a good chef's knife, paring knife, serrated slicer and a vegetable peeler.
- Covered jars for storage.
- An electric mixer.
- A grater and chopping board.
- A 6-cup muffin tin.
- An electric grill with two sides
- 10-12 ounce microwave and oven-safe custard cups or ramekins.
- A 2½ quart slow cooker.
- A can opener

Essential Tips

1. Fruits and vegetables are healthier and tastes better when consumed fresh; you don't have to store them up for long. So get smaller quantities of to avoid spoilage. If you can, buy them at fruit stands rather than the pre-packed ones at the grocery store. That way, you can pick the exact quantities you will need.

2. Make a list of leftovers and make-ahead meals that are kept in the fridge and paste it on the fridge. The list should also contain the maximum number of days the food can keep up and ensure to use it before that date. This will go a long way in preventing food wastage and clearing up your fridge for more space.

3. Food items that are not going to be used in weeks or months can be transferred to the freezer. Food like butter, bread and other pastries, and vegetables like peas and spinach and be kept frozen for months and thawed whenever they are to be used.

4. Canned foods like beans, tomatoes, can stay on the pantry shelf but are best preserved in the refrigerator once they are opened. Same goes for ketchup, mustards and other sauces. It is best to keep already ripe fruits in the fridge to prevent them from further ripening.

Best Places To Keep Your Food Items In The Kitchen

REFRIGERATOR	FREEZER	PANTRY
Eggs	Broth/ Stock	Kosher salt
Butter	Sausage	Ground dry pepper
Milk and yogurts	Bacon	Garlic
Dijon mustard	Shrimp	Onions
Carrots and broccoli	Spinach/Peas	Potatoes
Parsley	Ground beef/ turkey	Rice/quinoa
Cheese e.g. parmesan, cheddar	Chicken	Dried lentils
Opened canned foods	Fish	Pasta/ spaghetti
Maple syrup	Pork	Olive oil
Grapes		Cooking oil
Soy and nut milk		Vinegar
Ripe fruits e.g. bananas, avocados		Peanut butter
Ketchup and sauces		Soy sauce
Horseradish		Canned beans
		Fruits like apples, peaches, pears, lemons
		Dried beans
		Vegetables like eggplant, tomatoes
		Unripe bananas, avocados
		Bread

BREAKFAST

Creamy Dominican Oatmeal

Preparation: 10 minutes

Cooking time: 5 minutes

Ingredients:

½ cup fast cooking oats

1½ cups milk

¼ tsp ground cinnamon

2 tsp white sugar

1 pinch ground nutmeg

1 pinch salt

Directions:

1. Place the cinnamon, salt, nutmeg, sugar and milk in a saucepan.

2. Allow the mixture to boil, while you keep stirring continuously for about 2 minutes.

Creamy Potato-Bacon Skillet

Preparation: 10 minutes

Cooking time: 30 minutes

Ingredients:

4 slices of bacon

2 potatoes, peeled, diced

1/8 tsp seasoned salt

1/8 tsp garlic salt

1/8 tsp black pepper

3 eggs, whisked

4 tbsp shredded Cheddar cheese

Directions:

1. Get a deep, large skillet and place the bacon in it over medium-high heat; cook until evenly brown.

2. Take out the bacon slices; keep the dripping for later use. Crumble the cooked bacon and then keep aside.

3. Combine the diced potatoes with the reserved bacon grease; add black pepper, garlic salt and seasoned salt. Cook until the potatoes become tender and then add the crumbled bacon; cover with the whisked eggs.

4. Cook until it becomes firm. Spread the cheese on top and cover until it melts.

Porridge Brown Rice

An ingenious way to use your left over brown rice.

Preparation: 5 minutes

Cooking time: 25 minutes

Ingredients:

1 cup low-fat milk

1 cup cooked brown rice

2 tbsp dried blueberries or any mixture of dried fruit

¼ tsp vanilla extract

1 tbsp butter

1 tbsp honey

1 dash cinnamon

1 egg

Directions:

1. Get a small saucepan and place the blueberries or dried fruit, cinnamon, honey, milk and the brown rice all in it; mix to blend.

2. Bring to boil, and then turn down heat to low; allow to simmer for about 20 minutes.

3. In a bowl, whisk the egg and temper by stirring in some rice mixture, 1 tbsp per time, until about 6 tbsp have been added.

4. Pour the egg mixture back into the hot rice and add the butter and vanilla; stir to mix and keep cooking for 1 to 2 minutes over low heat until thick.

Mushroom 'N' Spinach Omelet

This is the best omelet I have ever tasted. Try it!

Preparation: 15 minutes

Cooking time: 15 minutes

Ingredients:

3 egg whites

1 egg

1 tbsp shredded cheddar cheese

1 tbsp grated parmesan cheese

1/8 tsp ground black pepper

1/8 tsp garlic powder

1/8 tsp red pepper flakes

1/8 tsp ground nutmeg

¼ tsp salt

¼ cup diced green onion

1 cup shredded fresh spinach

½ cup sliced fresh mushrooms

½ cup diced fresh tomato

½ tsp olive oil

2 tbsp finely chopped red bell pepper

Directions:

1. Place the egg whites and egg in a bowl and beat thoroughly. Add in the cheddar and parmesan cheese, salt, nutmeg, garlic powder, red pepper flakes and pepper.

2. Pour oil into a large skillet and heat over medium heat; add the green onion, bell pepper and mushrooms. Stir-fry for about 5 minutes until tender. Add the spinach and continue cooking until it wilts.

3. Mix in egg mixture and diced tomatoes and stir. When the eggs begins to set, raise the edges to allow the uncooked parts to flow under and cook properly. Continue cooking for 10 to 15 minutes until the egg mixture fully sets.

4. Cut it into wedges and serve immediately with preferred fruit and whole grain toast.

Shredded Cheese Potato Blend

These fantastic cheesy potatoes can be eaten alone or as a side dish to any main breakfast dish.

Preparation: 5 minutes

Cooking time: 10 minutes

Ingredients:

2 potatoes, peeled and cut into slices

¼ tsp salt

¼ cup sliced onion

¼ tsp garlic salt

1/8 tsp pepper

4 tbsp shredded cheddar cheese

Directions:

1. Get a 9" microwave-safe bowl and coat with cooking spray.

2. Set the potato and onion slices on the bowl; sprinkle with the seasonings.

3. Set microwave to high heat, cover the bowl and microwave until the potatoes are tender for about10 minutes.

4. Add cheese 30 seconds before cooking time elapse.

Chips And Peanut Butter Pancake

Crunchy and great-tasting. You would always want to make your pancakes this way.

Preparation: 10 minutes

Cooking time: 5 minutes

Ingredients:

1 tbsp sugar

¾ cup pancake mix

1 egg, lightly beaten

½ cup milk

1/3 cup peanut butter chips

¼ cup chopped pecans

¼ cup chopped pecans

Fresh strawberries and pancake syrup

Directions:

1. Put the pancake mix and the sugar into a big bowl. Mix the milk and the egg in a smaller bowl.

2. Pour the egg mixture into the dry pancake mixture; stir together until blended and moist. Fold in the nuts and chips.

3. Pour ¼ cup of the batter for each pancake, over a oiled hot griddle. When each pancake becomes bubbly on top, flip to reverse side and cook until golden brown.

5. Serve garnished with strawberries and syrup.

Nuts 'N' Berries Banana Splits

Nutritious, easy to prepare and so delicious.

Preparation: 10 minutes

Cooking time: 0 minute

Ingredients:

1 medium-sized banana

1/3 cup fresh strawberries, halved

1/3 cup seedless grapes, halved

1/3 cup fresh blueberry

1/3 cup kiwifruit, peeled and sliced

1 cup vanilla yogurt

2 maraschino cherries with stems

½ cup granola with fruit and nuts

Directions:

1. Get a knife and cut banana crosswise in half.

2. To serve, cut each fruit half along the length and place in two serving plates. Top each serving with the remaining ingredients.

Potato Mushroom Omelet

There is never a dull moment at breakfast anytime this exciting and colorful omelet is served.

Preparation: 8 minutes

Cooking time: 12 minutes

Ingredients:

¼ cup sliced fresh mushrooms

2 small red potatoes, diced

1 tbsp chopped green pepper

1 green onion, chopped

1 tbsp chopped sweet red pepper

1 tbsp olive oil

¼ cup shredded cheddar cheese, divided

2 tbsp sour cream

2/3 cup egg substitute

¼ cup chopped tomato

Directions

1. Bring a saucepan of potatoes covered with water to boil. Turn down heat and cook covered until soft, for 5 to 7 minutes and then drain.

2. Put the oil in a skillet and sauté the onion, mushrooms, potatoes and peppers until soft.

3. Apply cooking spray to another skillet and heat on medium flame. Add the egg substitute. When the eggs begin to set, push the edges to the middle allowing the uncooked parts to flow underneath. When everything sets, scoop some of the vegetable mixture on top; top with 2 tbsp shredded cheese.

4. Place on a serving dish and top with the remaining cheese, sour cream and tomato.

Broccoli Cheese Quiches

Preparation: 10 minutes

Cooking time: 20 minutes

Ingredients:

½ cup fresh or frozen broccoli florets, thawed and drained

1 bacon strip, cooked and crumbled

½ cup half-and-half cream

½ cup shredded Swiss cheese

2 eggs

1/8 teaspoon salt

1 dash lemon-pepper seasoning

1 dash garlic powder

Directions:

1. Get two 5" pie plates and coat with cooking spray.

2. Share the bacon, broccoli and cheese between the two plates.

3. Beat the cream, eggs, garlic powder, lemon-pepper and salt in a bowl and then pour the mixture over the bacon.

4. Bake at 350°F, uncovered, for 15 to 20 minutes until a knife inserted comes out clean.

Cheesy And Spicy Potato Pizza

Preparation: 20 minutes

Cooking time: 25 minutes

Ingredients:

¼ lb pork sausage roll or 4 pork sausage links, sliced

4-oz tube refrigerated crescent rolls

2 tbsp diced sweet red pepper

½ cup shredded hash brown potatoes

2 tbsp diced green pepper

2 eggs

½cup shredded cheddar cheese

2 tbsp milk

1/8 teaspoon pepper

1 tbsp shredded Parmesan cheese

Directions:

1. Arrange the crescent dough separately into 4 triangles on a 7½" ungreased round pizza pan with the points towards the middle. Press the dough onto the pan to build up the edges slightly.

2. Place a skillet over medium heat and cook the sausage until it changes from pink, then drain. Sprinkle the cooked sausage over the crust. Top with peppers, cheddar cheese and potatoes.

3. Beat eggs, pepper and milk in a bowl; pour the egg mixture over pizza and sprinkle with the cheese.

4. Place in an oven at 375°F; bake until the top becomes golden brown and eggs are totally set, about 20 to 25 minutes. Slice the pizza and serve.

Brown Rice Pudding

Preparation: 1 minute

Cooking time: 15 minutes

Ingredients:

1 cup milk

1½ cups cooked brown rice (cold)

1 banana (½ sliced, ½ mashed,)

1 tbsp butter

2 tbsp honey

½ tsp ground cinnamon

To garnish: extra honey, nuts, dried fruits

Directions:

1. Mix milk, brown rice, cinnamon and butter in a saucepan over low heat; stir thoroughly together. Allow to simmer while occasionally stirring.

2. Add the honey and mashed banana; cook for 1 minute until thickened.

3. Serve into two bowls; top with the remaining banana slices and any other garnish like honey nuts or dried fruits.

SNACKS AND APPETIZERS

Tenderloin Cheese Strips

Preparation: 15 minutes

Cooking time: 15 minutes

Ingredients:

1 (8-oz) pork tenderloin, cut into ½" pieces

¼ cup crumbled buttered crackers

3 tbsp butter, melted

½ tsp dried basil leaves

2 tbsp grated parmesan

¼ tsp pepper

¼ tsp salt

Marinara sauce (optional)

Directions:

1. Mix the cheese, crackers crumbs, pepper, basil and salt together in a flat bowl. Put the melted better in another a flat bowl. Put the pork into the butter to coat and then press into the crumb mixture to coat.

2. Line a baking sheet with foil (no need to grease); place the crumb coated tenderloin on the sheet and bake for10 to 15 minutes at 400°F until the juice is clear.

3. Remove from oven and serve along with marinara sauce, if preferred.

Spiral Dill Bites

These savory snacks are very easy to put together and very tasty.

Preparation: 15 minutes (plus 1 hour chilling time)

Cooking time: 0 minute

Ingredients:

2 (8-inch) flour tortillas

6 large spinach leaves

6 thin tomato slices

3 oz cream cheese, softened

1 tbsp trimmed fresh dill

1 tbsp minced chives

Directions:

1. Mix the cheese, dill and chives together in a bowl until well combined.

2. Spread 1 tbsp of the mixture on each tortilla; add the tomato slices and spinach in layers on each tortilla spread. Top with the remaining dill mixture.

3. Roll the tortillas firmly and place in a plastic bag. Place in a fridge to chill for about an hour; remove from bag and slice each roll into four. Serve.

Grill Lime Shrimp With Cilantro Avocado Dip

One bite into this juicy and spicy shrimp will keep your appetite stirred up.

Preparation: 15 minutes

Cooking time: 5 minutes

Ingredients:

For the grilled shrimp:

8 oz shrimp, peeled, deveined

2 tbsp fresh lime + more for drizzling

1½ tbsp jalapeno, minced

1½ tbsp olive oil

¾ tbsp honey

1 dash salt

1 dash pepper

For the avocado dip:

¼ cup mashed avocado

2 tbsp non-fat plain Greek yogurt

¼ cup roughly chopped cilantro

1 tsp lime juice

1 tbsp minced garlic

Pepper to taste

Salt to taste

Directions:

1. Combine all the shrimp ingredients (except the shrimp) in a bowl and mix thoroughly. Add the shrimp; toss to coat evenly and cover. Place in a refrigerator to marinate for not less than 2 hours.

2. Heat up a grill to medium high and coat lightly with cooking spray. Put 4-5 shrimps onto each presoaked bamboo skewer (or any other skewer).

3. Place the skewered shrimps on the hot grill and cook for 1½ to 2 minutes until slightly charred. Turn the shrimps over and cook until slightly charred. Cover the grilled shrimps and keep warm.

4. Put the avocado, cilantro, lime juice, yogurt and garlic into a food processor and process until smooth; stop at intervals to scrape the sides of the bowl. Add pepper and salt to taste.

5. Drizzle some lime juice on the grilled shrimp and serve along with the cilantro avocado dip.

Corn And Black Bean Quesadillas

Preparation: 10 minutes

Cooking time: 15 minutes

Ingredients:

4 large tortillas

¼ orange or red bell pepper, chopped

¼ small onion, chopped

¼ cup salsa

½ tsp chili powder

½ tsp cumin

2 tsp butter

2 cups shredded cheese (cheddar, Monterrey jack or Colby)

1 tsp brown sugar

1 tsp olive oil

1 can black beans, drained and rinsed

1 small garlic clove, minced

1 full cup of corn (canned or thawed)

For serving: sour cream

Directions:

1. Heat the olive oil over medium-high heat in a skillet. Put in the bell pepper and onion; sauté until soft for 1 to 2 minutes. Add the garlic and cook for 30 seconds.

2. Put in the salsa, black beans, brown sugar, corn, chili powder and cumin; mix until well combined and turn down heat.

3. In another skillet, melt 1 tsp butter. Put a tortilla in it and then sprinkle some cheese over it. Add a full scoop of the corn and bean mixture and level it out in a layer; sprinkle more cheese over it. Top with another tortilla.

4. Cook the quesadilla until the tortilla at the bottom is golden and most of the cheese is melted. Gently flip over to the reverse side using a big spatula and cook until the tortilla at the bottom is golden and all the cheese is melted.

5. Repeat steps 3 and 4 for the other quesadilla. Serve along with some salsa and sour cream.

White Bean And Cheese Dip

Preparation: 35 minutes

Cooking time: 0 minute

Ingredients:

½ cup reduced fat 2% cottage cheese

15 oz cannellini bean, rinsed and drained

1 tbsp apple cider vinegar

2 tsp olive oil

½ tsp dried thyme

Freshly ground black pepper

Kosher salt

1 pinch smoked paprika

For garnish: chopped chives

Directions:

1. In a food processor, mix the vinegar, cheese, beans, thyme, pepper and salt; puree, scraping down at intervals until smooth.

2. Place in a refrigerator for 30 to 60 minutes to chill. Pour into two bowls, drizzle olive oil and sprinkle paprika on top. Garnish with the chopped chives.

Creamy Almond Spread

This is one cheese spread you would love to have anytime.

Preparation: 10 minutes

Cooking time: 0 minute

Ingredients:

2 tbsp mayonnaise

1 tbsp almond slices

1 green onion, chopped

½ cup shredded white cheddar cheese

1/8 tsp onion powder

1 dash Louisiana hot sauce

1 dash pepper

Assorted crackers or celery ribs

Directions:

1. Combine the cheese, mayonnaise, pepper, hot sauce and onion powder in a bowl. Add the almonds and green onion; stir to combine.

2. Cover with a lid and place in a refrigerator for a minimum of 4 hours. Serve with the crackers or celery. Enjoy!

Scallop And Pureed Carrot Spoons

Warm your taste buds with this stylish appetizer recipe.

Preparation: 20 minutes

Cooking time: 21 minutes

Ingredients:

1 large carrot, peeled, washed and cut into slices

6 scallops

1 tsp heavy cream

6 sprigs of fresh cilantro

1 dash of ras el hanout

Coriander (stems and leaves)

Olive oil

Pepper

Salt

Directions:

1. In a bowl, combine the scallops with ½ tsp olive oil, 1 dash of salt and 1 dash of ras el hanout and place in a fridge to marinate.

2. Cook the carrots with water or steam for 20 minutes until tender. Add the coriander, cream, pepper and salt to taste. Share puree in six appetizer spoons. Leave to cool.

3. Place a skillet over heat; put in the marinated scallops and allow to brown for about 1 minute. When the scallops are cooled, place one each on the pureed carrot in each spoon. Garnish with a sprig of cilantro.

Crispy Coconut Shrimps With Jam Chili Sauce

Preparation: 20 minutes

Cooking time: 15 minutes

Ingredients:

10 large shrimps, peeled, deveined and rinsed

3 tbsp unsweetened coconut flakes

3 tbsp panko breadcrumbs

1 tbsp flour

1 tbsp sweet chili sauce

1 tbsp pineapple/mango jam or preserves

1 dash chili powder

1 dash cayenne pepper

1 small egg or ½ large egg, whisked

Directions:

1. Prepare your baking sheet; line it with parchment or foil and coat with cooking spray. Heat up your oven to 425°F.

2. Mix panko breadcrumbs, cayenne pepper, chili powder and coconut flakes in a Ziploc bag; shake the bag to combine and keep aside.

3. Put the egg and the flour in two small bowls. In two batches, dredge the shrimps in the flour and then in the whisked egg; place in the Ziploc bag and shake until coated with the breadcrumbs-coconut mixture.

4. Place the coated shrimps on the prepared baking sheet; coat lightly with cooking spray. Bake until the coconut starts to brown and the shrimps become firm to touch, about 10 minutes.

5. In a microwave-safe bowl, mix the jam and chili sauce together; heat for 30 seconds on high or 5 minutes on medium-low temperature. Remove and stir; serve with the coconut shrimps.

Seared Vindaloo-Veggie Shrimp

Preparation: 5 minutes

Cooking time: 16 minutes

Ingredients:

2 tbsp extra virgin olive oil, divided

½ lb shrimp, peeled and divided

1 tbsp vindaloo seasoning

1 carrot, chopped into bite-sized pieces

½ red onion, thinly sliced

½ head of broccoli, broken into florets and trimmed

3 garlic cloves, minced

½ bunch collard greens, roughly chopped

½ bunch kale, roughly chopped

Freshly ground pepper

Coarse salt

Directions:

1. Clean the shrimp and then season with vindaloo seasoning.

2. Pour 1 tbsp oil in a skillet and heat. Add shrimp to heated oil, then sear on the side for about 3 minutes. Flip over and sear for 1-2 minutes. Remove from skillet and keep aside covered.

3. Pour the remaining oil into the pan; add the chopped carrots and sliced onions and sauté for 5 minutes, until they begin to soften. Add garlic and

broccoli, then sauté for additional 3 minutes. Season with the pepper and salt.

4. Now, add the greens and sauté for 3 minutes until wilted. If preferred, add more vindaloo seasoning to suite your taste.

5. Place the shrimps back into the skillet and toss thoroughly to mix.

6. Serve immediately and enjoy!

Thai Flavored Sea Bass En Papillote

Preparation: 15 minutes

Cooking time: 25 minutes

Ingredients:

12 new potatoes, cleaned

2 small sea bass, scaled and gutted

1 small knob salted butter

For the stuffing:

3½ oz chunk fresh ginger

2 lemon grass stalks

3 small red chilies, finely chopped

3 garlic cloves

Zest and juice of 1 lime, plus extra wedges to serve (optional)

To serve: coriander leaves

Directions:

1. Preheat oven to 356°F.

2. To make the stuffing; bruise the lemon grass by smashing with the blunt edge of a knife and then slice thinly into rings. Cut the ginger into fine slices across the grain. Crush the garlic, unpeeled to release their fragrance. Mix all stuffing ingredients together in a bowl.

3. Place the 2 sea bass across the width of a 20-inch baking parchment. Take ¾ of the stuffing and fill the stomach cavities; spread the rest over the fish, then season afterwards. The sides of the baking parchment should be folded over the fish's heads and tails; roll into a neatly packed parcel. Refrigerate for a couple of hours until ready to cook.

4. To cook; place fish on an oven tray and then bake until the flesh scales off the bone, about 25 minutes.

5. Meanwhile, place the potatoes in water and boil until cooked. Drain properly, slice into two and put back in the pan with the butter.

6. Set the new potatoes and sea bass (if you wish, you can leave it still wrapped) on a serving plate and top with coriander.

Horseradish Trout

Preparation: 5 minutes

Cooking time: 20 minutes

Ingredients:

2 whole rainbow trout, gutted and cleaned

1 tbsp olive oil

1 lemon, thinly sliced

Sprigs of assorted herbs (thyme, dill and parsley would do)

To serve: fresh horseradish, grated,

Directions:

1. Preheat oven to 392°F.

2. Place trout on slightly greased baking sheet and fill the fish cavity with the herbs and sliced lemon. Season lavishly and drizzle with remaining oil.

3. Place fish in oven and allow to bake until the fish is thoroughly cooked, about 20 minutes (the flesh should be tender and the fish eyes should become very white).

4. Peel off the top skin layer and top with the grated horseradish. Serve garnished with any fresh vegetable of your choice.

Saffron Seafood Pasta

Treat yourself to this shellfish dinner enjoy the savory taste of the sea.

Preparation: 25 minutes

Cooking time: 25 minutes

Ingredients:

3 firm and fresh tomatoes

7 oz fusilli lunghi or another thin, long pasta

2 tbsp olive oil

3 garlic cloves, thinly sliced

3½ oz very large scallop, halved

3½ oz king prawn, deveined

10½ oz mussel, shells cleaned

3/5 cup white wine

1 pinch saffron, mixed with 3 tbsp hot water

4 tbsp single cream

Zest of 1 lemon, plus juice ½

2 tbsp pine nuts, toasted

1 small pack parsley, chopped

Directions:

1. Bring salted water in a large pan to boil; set aside a bowl with cold water in it.

2. Cut a little cross at the bottom of each tomato and then place them in the hot water. Transfer the tomatoes into the bowl of cold water with a slotted spoon after 15 seconds. (Keep the water boiling to cook the pasta).

3. Allow tomatoes to cool for about 30 seconds, and then remove. Use a sharp knife to remove the skin, start at the crossed base of each tomato. Slice each tomato into four; pull out and discard all its seeds and membrane. Dice the tomatoes and keep aside.

4. Add pasta to boiling water and cook for 2 minutes less than the time on the pack. In the meantime, heat the oil in large pan; add garlic and sauté until about to turn golden, about 2 minutes and then push to the edge of pan.

5. Turn up heat and put in the scallops and prawns; fry for 1 to 2 minutes or until scallops begin to turn golden and the prawns turn pink. Remove from pan and transfer to a plate.

6. Put the saffron along with its liquid, mussels, white wine and seasoning into the pan. Cover with lid and allow to steam until the mussels open up, about 3 minutes (throw away mussels that stay closed).

7. Add the cream, juice and lemon zest to the sauce; taste and adjust seasoning, as required. Drain the almost cooked pasta and add to the sauce with the scallops, diced tomato and prawns. Mix together and cook for an extra 2 minutes. Add parsley and pine nuts mix together again and serve.

Maple Glazed Spicy Salmon Filets

A lovely fish meal best foe weeknight dinner.

Preparation: 5 minutes

Cooking time: 18 minutes

Ingredients:

2 6-oz wild salmon filets

1 tbsp soy sauce

1 tbsp pure maple syrup

1 tsp Dijon mustard

1 garlic clove, minced

1 tsp chili powder

¼ tsp cayenne pepper

Directions:

1. Preheat oven to 350°F.

2. Place a parchment paper on a baking sheet to prevent the glazed fish from burning. Then place the salmon filets on the parchment paper separating them about 2" apart.

3. To make the glaze; whisk the Dijon mustard, maple syrup, chili powder, soy sauce, garlic and cayenne pepper together in a bowl. Brush the glaze generously over the salmon; reserve 2 tbsp for further glazing after the salmon is cooked.

4. Bake salmon for about 15 to 20 minutes or until salmon is properly baked. As a test of doneness, the salmon will flake with a fork. Take out from the oven and pour the reserved glaze over it. Serve with Brussels sprout and kale salad or sweet potato fries garnished with vegetables.

Baked Marinated Salmon

You can't go wrong with this very easy to make spicy salmons.

Preparation: 15 minutes (plus 1 hour marinating time)

Cooking time: 45 minutes

Ingredients:

2 6-oz salmon fillets

2 garlic cloves, minced

6 tbsp olive oil

1 tsp salt

1 tsp dried basil

1 tsp ground black pepper

1 tbsp chopped fresh parsley

1 tbsp lemon juice

Directions:

1. Prepare marinade in a glass bowl, by mixing lemon juice, garlic, basil, olive oil, parsley, pepper and salt.

2. Put the salmon fillets into a baking dish, and cover with the already prepared marinade. Place in a refrigerator to marinate for an hour, while turning occasionally.

3. Preheat oven to 375°F.

4. Wrap salmon fillets coated with the marinade, in an aluminum foil; place in a baking dish, and bake for 35-40 minutes, until it flakes with a fork.

Grilled Tilapia Salsa

Nothing tastes better than a tasty grilled tilapia topped with a juicy mango salsa. Yummy!

Preparation: 25 minutes (plus 1 hour of marinating)

Cooking time: 10 minutes

Ingredients:

2 6-oz tilapia fillets

1 tbsp minced fresh parsley

1/3 cup extra-virgin olive oil

1 tbsp lemon juice

1 tsp dried basil

1 garlic clove, minced

1 tsp ground black pepper

½ tsp salt

½ red bell pepper, diced

1 large ripe mango, peeled, pitted and diced

1 tbsp chopped fresh cilantro

2 tbsp minced red onion

1 jalapeno pepper, seeded and minced

1 tbsp lemon juice

2 tbsp lime juice

Pepper to taste

Salt to taste

Directions:

1. In a bowl, whisk the parsley, 1 tbsp lemon juice, extra-virgin olive oil, basil, 1 tsp pepper, garlic, and ½ tsp salt together and pour into a Ziploc bag. Put the tilapia into the bag and shake to coat with the marinade; squeeze to remove excess air, and then seal.

2. Place in the refrigerator to marinate for 1 hour.

3. In a bowl, prepare the salsa by mixing the red onion, mango, red bell pepper, jalapeno pepper and cilantro. Pour in 1 tbsp of lemon juice and the lime juice, and then toss to mix. Season as desired, with pepper and salt. Place in a refrigerator until about to serve.

3. Heat-up an outdoor grill to medium-high and oil the grate lightly.

4. Remove the tilapia from the marinade shaking off excess; throw away the remaining marinade. Set the fillets on grill cook each side for 3 - 4 minutes until the fish flakes with a fork and is no longer translucent at the middle. Top the tilapia with the salsa and serve.

Tips: Grilling time depends on how thick the fillets are.

Basil 'N' Shrimp Stuffed Eggplant

Preparation: 30 minutes

Cooking time: 45 minutes

Ingredients:

8 medium shrimps, peeled, deveined and chopped

½ cup olive oil, divided

1 eggplant, halved lengthwise

Salt and pepper to taste

2 tbsp chopped fresh basil

½ cup white wine

2 garlic cloves, chopped

½ cup grated Parmesan cheese, divided

1 cup Italian seasoned bread crumbs

Directions:

1. Heat oven to 350°F.

2. Scoop out the inner fleshy part of the eggplant, chop into bits, and set aside. Coat the eggplant shells with olive oil, add pepper and salt to taste and then keep aside.

3. Pour ¼ cup olive oil into a large skillet and place over medium-high heat. Add the garlic, shrimps and basil for a minute until the shrimps become pink. Put in the chopped eggplant; add pepper and salt to taste, and stir. Add the wine and allow to cook for 5 minutes.

4. Remove from heat and pour into a large bowl; add ¼ cup parmesan and breadcrumbs and stir to mix. If the mixture feels dry, add more olive oil and stir. Fill the eggplant shells with the mixture, and sprinkle the remaining parmesan cheese on top.

4. Place in the hot oven and bake until the eggplant is soft, about 30-40 minutes.

Buttered Shrimp Scampi

Preparation: 20 minutes

Cooking time: 15 minutes

Ingredients:

30 medium size shrimps, peeled and divided

2 tbsp butter, melted

2 tbsp olive oil

2 garlic cloves, minced

¼ tsp ground black pepper

½ tsp kosher salt

Directions:

1. Preheat oven to 350°F.

2. In a bowl, combine the shrimps, melted butter, salt, olive oil, garlic and pepper; toss and allow to stand for about 10 minutes.

3. Set the shrimp around the edges of a casserole dish. Put into the hot oven and bake for 15 minutes until the shrimps turn pink and are cooked through.

Lemon Flavored Stuffed Lobster Tails

This exquisite meal is a great family delight.

Preparation: 20 minutes

Cooking time: 10 minutes

Ingredients:

2 lobster tails, split along the center top

2 tsp butter, melted

½ cup jumbo lump crabmeat

15 buttery round crackers, crushed

¼ cup clarified butter

1 tbsp chopped fresh parsley leaves

1 tsp seafood seasoning

1 clove garlic, minced

1 tbsp fresh lemon juice

1 tsp lemon zest

¼ tsp freshly ground white pepper

¼ tsp salt

Directions:

1. Preheat oven to 425°F.

2. Lift the tail meat carefully, to rest above the shells, after pulling apart the sides of the lobster shells. Set the lobster tails on a baking sheet. Use 1 tsp of melted butter to brush each portion of the tail meat.

3. Thoroughly mix the crabmeat, crushed crackers, parsley, 1/4 cup of clarified butter, garlic, seafood seasoning, lemon zest, white pepper, lemon juice and salt in a bowl.

5. Scoop half the stuffing mixture into each lobster tail; press slightly to shape stuffing and to prevent it from falling off.

6. Place lobster tails in the hot oven and bake for 10 to 12 minutes until the stuffing turns golden brown on top and the flesh is no longer transparent. Locate the thickest part of the lobster tail and insert an instant-read thermometer; this should read 145°F to proof doneness. Serve and Enjoy!

Grilled Smoky Hamburgers

Preparation: 5 minutes

Cooking time: 10 minutes

Ingredients:

1 lb lean ground beef

1 tbsp liquid smoke flavoring

1 tbsp Worcestershire sauce

1 tbsp olive oil

1 tsp garlic powder

Salt to taste

Directions:

1. Preheat grill to high heat.

2. Mix the liquid smoke, ground beef, garlic powder and Worcestershire sauce together in a medium size bowl.

3. Mold into 4 small patties or 2 large ones; brush the two sides of each patty with oil, and add salt to taste.

3. Place patties on grill grate to cook. Grill each side for 5 minutes until properly done. Serve on buns and garnish with desired toppings.

Mushroom And Steak Kabob With Salad

Preparation: 30 minutes

Cooking time: 15 minutes

Ingredients:

½ lb boneless beef top loin steak

1 cup sliced small mushrooms

2 tbsp tamari-ginger sauce or soy sauce (or more to taste)

¼ tsp garlic powder

4 cups leafy romaine

1 tbsp olive oil

½ cup broccoli florets, cooked and cooled

½ cup julienne-cut carrots

Lite balsamic and caper vinaigrette

Directions:

1. Neatly slice steak into eight1" cubes. Thread four 6" skewers with two cubes of steak. Brush generously with sauce and place in a refrigerator for 15-20 minutes.

2. Remove steaks and discard the remaining sauce. Grill steak kabobs until well done.

3. Add the garlic powder to the mushrooms and mix. Heat oil in a nonstick skillet and sauté the seasoned mushrooms over medium-high heat. Sauté until slightly browned or for 4-5 minutes.

4. In a bowl, mix carrots, broccoli and romaine together; add enough lite balsamic and caper vinaigrette and toss.

5. Share the salad on 2 large dishes. Top each serving with steak kabobs and mushrooms. Store any leftover in the refrigerator.

Chinese Salad And Steak

Preparation: 20 minutes (plus 12 hours of marinating)

Cooking time: 10 minutes

Ingredients:

1 lb skirt steak, sliced into strips

2 tbsp soy sauce

¼ cup peanut oil

½ green bell pepper, chopped

1 tsp ground black pepper

¼ onion, chopped

1 tbsp chopped fresh ginger root

2 tbsp chopped green onion

1 cup fresh baby spinach

1 tbsp chopped Serrano pepper

¼ cup balsamic vinaigrette salad dressing

Directions:

1. In a small bowl, whisk soy sauce, peanut oil and pepper together; transfer the mixture into a Ziploc bag. Add the steak, shake to coat with marinade and squeeze to remove excess air; seal the bag. Place in a refrigerator for 12-24 hours to marinate.

2. Transfer the marinade and the steak into a skillet and place over medium heat; cook stirring regularly. Add the ginger, bell pepper, Serrano pepper, onion, green onion.

4. Continue cooking until the steak turns brown all round. Serve with the balsamic vinaigrette over a bed of spinach.

Harissa Lamb Couscous

Preparation: 30 minutes

Cooking time: 8 minutes

Ingredients:

4 lean lamb cutlets, fat trimmed

3½ oz non-fat Greek yogurt

1 tablespoonful harissa

For the couscous:

3½ oz couscous

14 oz can chickpea in water, drained

½ cup low-sodium vegetable stock, hot

1 tbsp white wine vinegar

Zest and juice of 1 lemon

6 dried apricot, chopped

1 small pack mint, chopped

1 small pack pomegranate seeds

Directions:

1. Preheat grill.

2. Combine half the harissa with seasoning and yogurt in a bowl. Take out 2 tbsp of the mixture and reserve for later use; put the lamb into the

remaining harissa mixture and marinate while preparing the couscous (or marinate overnight).

3. Soak the couscous in a bowl of hot stock and add the remaining harissa. Use cling film to cover the bowl and allow to stand for 5 minutes. Stir in the vinegar, chickpeas, lemon zest and juice, half the mint, apricots and pomegranate seeds.

4. Place the marinated lamb on a baking tray, then grill for 2 to 3 minutes per side. Add any cooking liquid from the lamb into the couscous and stir.

4. Serve lamb with couscous and top with the remaining mint and reserved harissa-yogurt.

Potato Lamb Rack Recipe

Preparation: 15 minutes

Cooking time: 40 minutes

Ingredients:

1 rack of lamb, French trimmed with the fat scored

1 onion, finely sliced

2 tbsp vegetable oil

14 oz new potato, sliced

3 garlic clove, finely sliced

½ bunch thyme (reserve a few sprigs to garnish)

4/5 cup chicken or lamb stock (preferably fresh)

To serve, asparagus (optional)

Directions:

1. Heat oven to 356°F. Heat a small roasting pan; coat lamb with 1 tbsp of oil and some salt.

2. Place lamb in the roasting pan, skin-side down, until the fat turns brown; sear the lamb all round. Remove from roasting pan and place on a plate.

3. Put the onion in the pan and cook until tender for 10 minutes. Add the thyme, potatoes, stock and garlic, then press down using a spoon.

4. Place the seared lamb on top and roast further in the hot oven for 25 to 30 minutes or until the lamb are well cooked and potatoes are soft.

5. Cover with foil and leave to stand for 10 minutes. Cut into cutlets and spread the reserved thyme sprigs over the cutlets. Serve with cooked asparagus and a scoop of the potatoes, if desired.

Beef Sautee With Polenta

Preparation: 20 minutes

Cooking time: 15 minutes

Ingredients:

For the marinade:

½ cup beef broth

3 garlic cloves, minced

¼ tsp ground black pepper

¼ tsp salt

½ rosemary sprig

1/8 tsp sugar

1-2 tbsp lemon juice

2-3 sage leaf

12-14 oz beef flank steak, sliced into strips

For the stir fry:

2-3 tbsp oil

½ red onion, sliced

2 garlic cloves

Salt and pepper to taste

4 tbsp marinade

Marinated beef flank steak

For the polenta:

2 cups milk or water

2 tsp salt (or as required)

1½ cup instant/quick-cooking cornmeal

1 tbsp butter

Cheese /sour cream or Greek yogurt (optional)

Directions:

1. Combine all the marinade ingredients in a re-sealable plastic bag; add the beef flank steak strips and shake the bag to coat the beef strips. Allow to marinate for 10 to 15 minutes or keep in the fridge overnight for a more enhanced flavor.

2. Meanwhile, make the polenta. Heat the milk or water, salt and butter in a saucepan until just about to boil. Measure the corn meal in a small bowl to make it easier to add in boiling water; turn down the heat.

3. When the water or milk is boiled, add the cornmeal slowly and whisking quickly. Keep whisking until the polenta becomes thick. Remove from heat but continue mixing; add more butter if required. Stir in Greek yoghurt, sour cream or cheese if desired. Cover and keep aside. All these are done in about 5 minutes.

4. For the stir-fry, heat oil over high heat; add the onion and garlic. Reduce the heat and allow the garlic and onion to flavor the oil, but don't let them get burnt. Remove the flank steak strips from the marinade and reserve some marinade (about 4 tablespoons) for stir fry.

5. Add the beef strips to the oil until slightly browned on the two sides. Put in the marinade and season with pepper and salt to taste. Allow to cook, covered, over medium high heat until about half of the marinade/liquid evaporates (about 5 minutes). Stir the beef a few more times.

6. Serve beef strips over creamy polenta and garnish with a sprig of rosemary.

Cubed Steak With Sherry And Mushroom Sauce

Looking for a quick weeknight dinner? Try these cubed steaks in a tasty mushroom and sherry sauce...and thank me later.

Preparation: 5 minutes

Cooking time: 20 minutes

Ingredients:

2 4-oz cube steaks

1 tbsp + 2 tsp extra virgin olive oil, divided

¼ tsp salt

⅜ tsp freshly ground pepper, divided

4 oz sliced mushrooms (about 1¼ cups)

½ large shallot, thinly sliced

½ tsp chopped fresh thyme or ⅛ teaspoon dried

1½ tsp all-purpose flour

¼ cup beef broth

¼ cup dry sherry

1 tbsp reduced-fat sour cream

Directions:

1. Put 1 tbsp oil in a oil in a nonstick skillet and place over medium heat. Season the steaks with ¼ tsp salt and pepper. Add steaks to the skillet and cook each side for 1-2 minutes until brown, turning once. Place on a plate with a lid and keep warm.

2. Pour the remaining 2 tsp oil to the skillet. Add shallot, mushrooms, and the remaining pepper; cook for 5 minutes, while stirring continuously, until the mushrooms release their liquid and turn golden brown. Sprinkle the flour over the mushrooms; cook and stir for another minute.

3. Put in the broth, thyme and sherry; bring to boil and cook for 2-3 minutes, stirring until thick and able to coat the back of a spoon. Take out from heat and stir in the sour cream. Put bake the steak and its juice in the skillet and stir to coat with sauce. Serve the steaks and sauce. Enjoy.

Tips: Sherry is originally produced from southern Spain and is a fortified wine. It's best to use the dry sherry sold in liquor stores for this recipe as it has less amount of sodium than the cooking sherry sold in supermarkets.

Chilied Steaks with Pan Salsa

Preparation: 5 minutes

Cooking time: 10 minutes

Ingredients:

8 oz (½-inch thick) steaks, fat trimmed and cut into two

½ tsp kosher salt, divided

1 tsp chili powder

2 plum tomatoes, diced

1 tsp extra virgin olive oil

1 tbsp chopped fresh cilantro

2 tsp lime juice

Directions:

1. Sprinkle ¼ tsp salt and chili powder on the two sides of the steak. Heat oil over medium-high heat in a skillet. Add the seasoned steaks and cook each side for 2 minutes turning once. Transfer the cooked steaks to a plate and cover with foil; keep aside.

2. To make the salsa; add lime juice, tomatoes, and remaining ¼ tsp salt to the skillet and cook for about 3 minutes, stirring regularly, until the tomatoes are soft. Turn off heat and mix in the cilantro and any juice from the steaks. Top the steaks with salsa and serve.

Mushroom-Topped Beef Fillets With Sauce

Enjoy this delicious and quick to prepare exquisite meal for lunch or dinner.

Preparation: 15 minutes

Cooking time: 15 minutes

Ingredients:

2 4-oz beef tenderloin steaks

1 tsp all-purpose flour

½ cup dry red wine or reduced-sodium beef broth

½ cup reduced-sodium beef broth

1 tsp Worcestershire sauce

1 tsp steak sauce

1 tsp ketchup

½ tsp ground mustard

1/8 tsp salt

¼ tsp pepper

4 oz fresh baby Portobello mushrooms, sliced

1 tsp minced chives (optional)

Directions:

1. Coat a large skillet with cooking spray.

2. Over medium-high heat, place steaks in skillet until browned on both sides. Remove from heat and keep warm.

3. Lower heat to medium. Pour the wine into the skillet and keep stirring to loosen up browned bits. Continue cooking until half of the liquid is left,

about 3 minutes. Add the flour and the broth until it becomes smooth; whisk in the juices from the steak. Add the Worcestershire sauce, steak sauce, mustard and ketchup and then bring to a boil.

3. Place steaks back in skillet and add mushrooms. Cook each side for 4 to 5 minutes until meat is properly cooked (a meat thermometer should read 338°F). Sprinkle with salt, chives and pepper as you choose.

MAIN DISH: CHICKEN

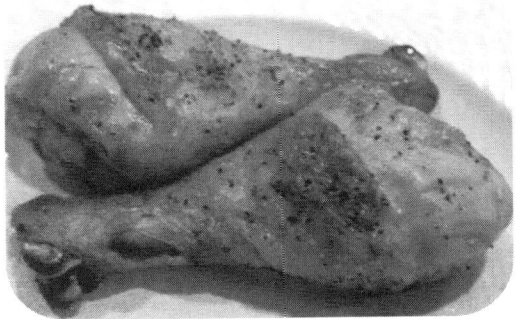

Breaded Hazelnut Chicken

Preparation: 10 minutes

Cooking time: 10 minutes

Ingredients:

4 skinless, boneless chicken breasts

1 cup dried breadcrumbs, seasoned

½ cup ground hazelnuts

8 fresh mushrooms, sliced

1 egg, beaten

1/8 cup butter

2 fl. oz hazelnut liqueur

1½ fl. oz brandy

Directions:

1. Mix the bread crumbs and hazelnuts together in a shallow dish. Dip the chicken in the beaten egg and then dredge in the breadcrumb-hazelnut mixture to coat.

2. Melt the butter over medium-high heat in a saucepan. Add chicken until brown on the two sides; add the mushrooms and more butter if required. Sauté for about 2 minutes, until mushrooms are soft.

3. Remove from heat and put in brandy. Light-up the mixture with a match and allow alcohol evaporate. As soon as the flame goes out, add hazelnut liquor. Light with a match and allow alcohol evaporate. Immediately the flame goes out, place the saucepan back over heat and allow to simmer until it gets thick. Ready to serve!

Lemon Herb Chicken Breast

Preparation: 10 minutes

Cooking time: 15 minutes

Ingredients:

2 skinless, boneless chicken breast halves

Salt and pepper to taste

1 tbsp olive oil

1 lemon

1 pinch dried oregano

2 sprigs fresh parsley, for garnish

Directions:

1. Cut lemon into two equal halves and squeeze the juice from one half lemon on chicken. Add salt to taste; allow to sit.

2. Heat oil in small skillet over medium-low heat. When hot, add the chicken and sauté. Squeeze in juice from the other lemon half; add oregano and pepper to taste.

3. Sauté each side for 5-10 minutes until juice runs clear. Garnish with parsley and serve hot.

Roasted Stuffed Guinea Fowl With Gravy

Preparation: 20 minutes

Cooking time: 1 hour 20 minutes

Ingredients:

1 small guinea fowl (about 2 lb)

8 streaky rasher bacon

2 tbsp plain flour

3½ tbsp soft butter

1½ cups strong chicken stock

1 onion, unpeeled and thickly sliced

Salt and pepper to taste

Sugar

For the stuffing:

1 onion, chopped

1 tbsp chopped sage

1¾ tbsp butter

1.7 oz walnut, finely chopped

3½ tbsp breadcrumb

¼ tsp ground mace

Zest of 2 lemons

3½ oz cooked chestnut, quartered

1 egg, beaten

Salt and pepper, to taste

To serve: roast potatoes, cranberry sauce and vegetables

Directions:

1. To prepare the stuffing; let the onion soften gently in butter. Add the sage, stir, and cook for another 2 minutes. Transfer into a bowl, then mix together with chopped walnuts, lemon zest, breadcrumbs, mace, chestnuts and egg. Season as required.

2. To prepare the guinea fowl; wash the inside cavity thoroughly. Mix butter with seasoning; spread some of it over the breasts, under the skin and apply the rest all over the legs. Place bacon across breasts, smoothing over as you apply, and season with more pepper as required.

3. Fill cavity with stuffing. Cover and refrigerate the guinea fowl not more than 24 hours if not using immediately. Bring the stuffed guinea fowl out of the fridge 30 minutes before use.

4. Set the temperature of your oven to 392°F. Put the thickly sliced onions in a roasting tin and place the fowl on it. Roast in hot oven for 15 minutes and then reduce the temperature to 356°F. Continue roasting for another 35 to 45 minutes. The fowl is properly cooked when the juices run clear when pierced with a knife.

5. Transfer the guinea fowl to a plate and wrap loosely with a foil and then a towel to preserve the heat. Set aside while you prepare the gravy.

6. To make the gravy; pour all the juices from the roasting tin into a bowl. Scoop out 1 tbsp of fat from the top layer of the juice into the roasting tin and place over low heat. Add the flour and stir until no longer dusty.

7. Scoop out the remaining fat from the meat juices and discard. Slowly stir in the juices and the stock and boil gently until becomes thick. Add pepper, salt and a little sugar, if needed; stain into a jug and throw the onions away.

8. Serve the stuffed guinea fowl with the gravy and cranberry sauce; garnish with lots of vegetables. Yummy!

Peppered Pineapple Chicken Barbeque

A delicious blend of pineapple, pepper and chicken.

Preparation: 15 minutes

Cooking time: 15 minutes

Ingredients:

½ lb skinless, boneless chicken breast halves, cut into 1" pieces

1 green bell pepper, cut into 1" pieces

15 oz pineapple chunks, drained

½ onion, cut into 1" pieces

¼ cup barbeque sauce (or more, as needed)

6 skewers

Directions:

1. Heat-up a grill for medium-high heat and oil the grate lightly.

2. Thread the chicken, pineapple, green bell pepper, and onion onto the skewers; brush generously with the barbeque sauce.

3. Place barbeque on the hot grill and cook for 7 to 10 minutes on each side, until the center of the chicken changes from pink and juices run clear.

Pesto Chicken Caprese Flatbread

Preparation: 10 minutes

Cooking time: 8 minutes

Ingredients:

2 large flatbreads

½ cup chopped/shredded chicken

4 oz fresh mozzarella, sliced

1-2 tbsp olive oil

1 tbsp pesto sauce

1 cup cherry tomatoes, sliced in half

¼ cup freshly grated parmesan cheese

1/3 cup chopped fresh basil (about 6-8 leaves)

Balsamic vinegar

Directions:

1. Preheat oven to 500°F.

2. Coat the flatbreads with olive oil; add shredded chicken in the pesto sauce and toss.

3. Place the mozzarella cheese, tomatoes and the pesto chicken in layers on each flatbread. Top with the grated parmesan cheese.

4. Place in hot open and bake until cheese melt and becomes bubbly, about 4 to 8 minutes. Take out of oven; top with chopped fresh basil leaves and drizzle of balsamic vinegar, as desired.

Lemon Baked Honey Chicken

Preparation: 15 minutes

Cooking time: 30 minutes

Ingredients:

2 chicken breasts

½ tbsp oil (or butter)

1 tbsp wholegrain mustard

1 tbsp Dijon mustard

1 tbsp honey

¼ tsp paprika

Salt and pepper, to taste

Juice from ½ lemon

Broccoli spears, to serve

Directions:

1. Set oven temperature to 400°F.

2. Oil an oven-safe dish with butter or oil and set the chicken in it.

3. Add salt, paprika and pepper to season.

4. Mix the honey, Dijon mustard and wholegrain mustard together in a small bowl.

5. Pour the mixture all over the chicken and bake for 30 to 45 minutes, depending on how big the chicken is. You can add to the dish, 1 to 2 tbsp of water (just in case the juices produced during baking is not much) to prevent the edges from browning.

7. Squeeze the lemon juice over the cooked chicken and serve, garnished with the broccoli spears.

Creamy Mushroom Chicken

Preparation: 10 minutes

Cooking time: 30 minutes

Ingredients:

2 boneless, skinless chicken breasts (5-oz each), trimmed and tenders removed

1 tbsp canola oil

¼ tsp salt

½ tsp freshly ground pepper

1 shallot, minced

1 cup shiitake mushroom caps, thinly sliced

¼ cup reduced-sodium chicken broth

2 tbsp heavy cream

2 tbsp dry vermouth or white wine (dry)

2 tbsp minced fresh chives, or scallion greens

Directions:

1. Season both sides of the chicken with salt and pepper.

2. Heat oil over medium heat in skillet. Add chicken and cook for 12-16 minutes until brown; turn occasionally and adjust heat to keep from burning. When cooked, the chicken should read 165°F. Place on a plate and wrap with foil to keep it warm.

3. Place the shallot into the pan and cook, for 30 seconds, stirring continuously until it gives off a sweet aroma. Put in the mushrooms; cook

and stir for 2 minutes until soft. Add the wine or vermouth and simmer for about a minute until the alcohol is almost evaporated.

4. Pour the broth in and cook for 1 to 2 minutes until reduced by about half, then stir in cream and scallions (or chives); continue to simmer. Put back the chicken to pan, coat with sauce, then cook for about 1 minute until heated through.

Tips: Remove the thin strip of meat (tenders) from underside of a 5-oz chicken breast. This removes 1 oz of meat and yields a perfect 4-oz portion. Freeze tenders and use them in a sauce, stir-fry or baked chicken fingers.

Orange Marmalade Chicken

Preparation: 10 minutes

Cooking time: 20 minutes

Ingredients:

1 lb chicken tenders

1 cup reduced-sodium chicken broth

2 tbsp red-wine vinegar

2 tbsp orange marmalade

1 tsp Dijon mustard

1 tsp cornstarch

¼ tsp freshly ground pepper

½ tsp kosher salt

2 tbsp extra-virgin olive oil, divided

1 tbsp freshly grated orange zest

2 large shallots, minced

Directions:

1. Mix marmalade, broth, cornstarch, mustard and vinegar in a bowl.

2. Sprinkle salt and pepper on chicken. In a large skillet, heat 4 tsp of oil over medium-high heat. Add chicken and cook for about 2 minutes on each side until it turns golden. Set on a plate and place foil over to keep warm.

3. Add the shallots and remaining 2 tsp of oil to pan; cook for about 30 seconds, while stirring often, till it begins to turn brown. Mix the broth mixture, add to pan and bring to a simmer; scrape up the browned bits.

4. Lower heat and keep simmering until sauce reduces slightly and becomes thick, about 30 seconds - 2 minutes. Add chicken and cook for another minute until chicken is well heated, turning once. Turn off the heat and stir in the orange zest. Serve along with brown rice.

Tip: Chicken tenders are fat-free rib meat strips that are attached beneath the chicken breasts. They are also sold separately in the store and are great for stir-fries or breaded chicken fingers

Baked Potato 'N' Chicken

Preparation: 20 minutes

Cooking time: 40 minutes

Ingredients:

2 chicken breast halves, boneless, skinless (about ½ lb)

¾ lb red potato, cut into quarters

2 tbsp Dijon mustard

½ cup bisquick mix

1 small onion, cut into 8 wedges

1 small bell pepper, cut into ½" pieces

½ tsp paprika

2 tbsp grated parmesan cheese (optional)

Directions:

1. Preheat oven to 400°F. Apply cooking spray on a 13x9x2-inch baking dish.

2. Coat the chicken with 1 tbsp of mustard and then with the bisquick mix. Use the remaining mustard to coat the onion, potatoes and bell pepper. Arrange the chicken at the corners of the pan; put the vegetables in the middle of the pan and spray both vegetables and chicken with the cooking spray. Sprinkle with paprika and cheese evenly.

3. Bake in the hot oven for 35-40 minutes until the potatoes are soft and the center of the chicken is no more pink Stir the vegetables 20 minutes through baking. Serve when ready.

SALADS

Feta-Watermelon Salad

Enjoy this light summer salad loaded with the freshness of berries, watermelon and a blend of balsamic vinaigrette.

Preparation: 10 minutes

Cooking time: 0 minute

Ingredients:

For the salad:

½ cup fresh berries (blackberries, blueberries and raspberries)

½ cup cubed watermelon

4 cups spring mix

3 tbsp chopped basil leaves

3 tbsp crumbled feta

For the Balsamic Vinaigrette:

4 tbsp canola oil

2 tbsp balsamic vinegar

1 tsp brown sugar

Directions:

1. To make the balsamic vinaigrette; mix the brown sugar and balsamic vinegar together in a bowl. Stir in the oil gently and slowly until the mixture is well blended and thick; keep aside until about to serve salad. Stir the minute again before pouring over salad.

2. To make the salad; divide the spring mix between two bowls. Top with the watermelons and then add the berries, feta and lastly the basil evenly in both bowls. Drizzle the vinaigrette over the salads and serve.

Healthy Detox Salad

Contains everything you'll need for a complete body detox.

Preparation: 15 minutes

Cooking time: 0 minute

Ingredients:

2 small beetroots, chopped

1 medium cucumber, seeded and chopped

4 celery stalks, chopped

½ avocado diced

½ cup red onions, chopped

2 cups any green vegetable of your choice (you can use mixed greens, baby arugula or spinach)

2 tbsp lemon juice

2 tbsp EVOO or flax oil

Kosher salt

Freshly ground black pepper

Directions:

1. Put the beetroots, celery, your greens, avocado, cucumber and onions into a big bowl and toss to mix.

2. Combine the oil and lemon juice in a smaller bowl; add the mixture to the salad and toss to mix. Put in the pepper and salt and then serve.

Tip: You can also use watercress, endives and dandelions in this recipe because they are great detox staples.

Carroty Lemon Salad

Sweet tasting carrots and dill dressed in a blend of scallion and tangy lemon.

Preparation: 10 minutes

Cooking time: 0 minute

Ingredients:

1 cup shredded carrots

1 tbsp finely chopped scallion

1½ tbsp chopped fresh dill

1 tbsp EVOO (extra virgin olive oil)

1 tbsp lemon juice

½ garlic clove, minced

Freshly ground pepper, to taste

Salt, to taste

Directions:

1. In a bowl, combine the oil, lemon juice, pepper and salt and then stir. Put in the dill, scallion and carrots and toss to combine well. Serve immediately or cover in a container and place in the fridge for not more than two days.

Sweet Vinegar Coleslaw

This coleslaw goes with virtually everything and you don't even need to add mayonnaise to it.

Preparation:10 minutes

Cooking time: 0 minute

Ingredients:

1 medium carrot, scrapped and grated

1½ cup shredded cabbage

¼ cup slivered red onion

1 tbsp canola oil

1 tbsp white wine vinegar

1 tsp granulated white sugar

1 tsp Dijon mustard

1 pinch salt

1 pinch celery seed

Directions:

1. Combine the oil, vinegar, salt, celery seed and mustard in a bowl; stir.

2. Put in the onion, cabbage and carrot; toss everything together to coat and serve.

Hazelnut And Apple Scallop Salad

Juicy and enhanced with sweet flavors.

Preparation: 30 minutes

Cooking time: 5 minutes

Ingredients:

2 tbsp finely chopped toasted hazelnut

6 scallops, without roe

½ green apple

A small handful of watercress

2 tbsp butter

2 tsp virgin rapeseed oil + more for drizzling

½ lemon, juiced

For the Hazelnut Dressing:

¾ cup hazelnut

2 tsp maple syrup

3 tbsp cider vinegar

Directions:

1. To prepare the hazelnut dressing; toast the hazelnut in a pan until they are golden. Turn the toasted nuts into a food processor and process for 5 to 10 minutes until it forms a smooth oily paste. Put in the maple syrup and vinegar; continue blending. Add about 2/3 cup of water to the paste while the food processor is still running and blend until smooth.

2. Slice the apples with a sharp knife into matchstick-like strips; add a little lemon juice while cutting to prevent the browning of the apples.

3. Place the hazelnuts in a flat dish. Melt the butter in a sauce pan and heat until it starts to foam but not brown. Put in the scallops and fry each side for about a minute. Take out the scallops and place on the hazelnuts to coat.

4. To assemble; scoop a little of the dressing in the middle of each serving dish and spread it out with the back of a spoon. Combine what's left of the lemon juice and the oil in a bowl; add the watercress and toss with some seasoning. Heap the watercress on each dressing, place the scallops about the watercress and arrange piles of the apple-matchsticks between the scallops. Drizzle oil over it and serve.

Easy Lettuce Salad

Preparation: 10 minutes

Cooking time: 0 minute

Ingredients:

2-3 cups shredded lettuce

For the dressing:

2 tbsp red wine vinegar

2 tbsp olive oil

½ tsp sugar

½ tsp Italian seasoning

¼ tsp salt

1/8 tsp pepper

1/8 tsp garlic powder

Directions:

1. To make the dressing; in a bowl, add all the ingredients and stir to mix.

2. Share the lettuce between two serving plates. Drizzle the dressing over the shredded lettuce and serve.

Cheese 'N' Bacon Broccoli Salad

Preparation: 10 minutes (plus 1 hour chilling time)

Cooking time: 0 minute

Ingredients:

4 bacon strips, cooked and crumbled

1½ cups fresh broccoli florets

¾ cup shredded cheddar cheese

¼ cup finely chopped onion

2 tbsp white vinegar

3 tbsp mayonnaise

1 tbsp sugar

Directions:

1. Put the cheese, broccoli, onion and bacon into a medium bowl and toss to combine.

2. Mix the vinegar, mayonnaise and sugar in a smaller bowl. Drizzle this mixture over the broccoli-bacon mixture; toss to combine.

3. Cover and place in a fridge for about 1 hour to cool, then serve.

Simple Pineapple Coleslaw

Preparation: 10 minutes (plus 2 hours chilling time)

Cooking time: 0 minute

Ingredients:

8 ounces crushed and unsweetened pineapples, drained

2½ cups shredded cabbage

4 tbsp mayonnaise

¼ tsp pepper

¼ tsp salt

Directions:

1. Combine the pineapples, cabbage, mayonnaise, salt and pepper in a medium bowl.

2. Cover and place in a fridge for about 2 hours to cool, then serve.

Mixed Vegetable Salad

Preparation: 20 minutes

Cooking time: 0 minute

Ingredients:

8 asparagus, steamed or blanched, chopped

4 cauliflower florets, steamed or blanched, cut into four

5 broccoli florets, steamed or blanched, cut into four

3 radishes, trimmed and cut into four

½ yellow bell pepper, seeded, cut into two and sliced thinly

½ red bell pepper, seeded, cut into two and sliced thinly

3 cups shredded mixed greens (e.g. green or red leaf lettuce, romaine, Boston or Bibb leaves), washed and dried

1 carrot, grated

2 scallions, both white and green parts chopped

Freshly ground black pepper, to taste

Kosher salt, to taste

1 big beefsteak tomato, sliced into 8 wedges

Salad dressing: any of blue cheese, poppy seed, thousand island or miso-sesame

Directions:

1. Combine all the salad ingredients except the tomato and dressing in a large serving dish; toss to mix. Drizzle with the salad dressing of your choice.

2. Add salt and pepper to the tomato wedges and garnish by placing the about the inner edges of the salad bowl. Ready to serve.

Farm-Fresh Salad and Dressing

Preparation: 15 minutes (1 hour chilling time)

Cooking time: 0 minute

Ingredients:

For the Dressing:

1½ tbsp white vinegar

1½ tbsp chopped fresh green onions

1 tbsp chopped flat-leaf parsley

½ tbsp chopped fresh chives

2 tbsp mayonnaise

¼ cup plain yogurt (fat-free)

½ tsp chopped tarragon

½ clove garlic, minced

1 tsp anchovy paste

1/8 tsp freshly ground black pepper

1 dash salt

For the salad:

4 cups shredded romaine lettuce

1 hard-boiled eggs, sliced into 4 wedges each

1 large tomatoes (about 1 lb.), sliced into 8 wedges each

¾cups chopped cooked chicken breast

½ cup trimmed watercress

¼ cup peeled and diced avocado

2 tbsp crumbled blue cheese

Directions:

1. To make the dressing; put all the ingredients for the dressing into a food processor and process until it becomes smooth. Refrigerate for an hour to chill before serving.

2. To make the salad: in a bowl, mix the watercress and lettuce together. Put 2 cups of the lettuce mixture on each of two serving plates. Divide the chicken, tomato wedges, egg wedges, avocado and cheese equally between the two serving plates. Drizzle ¼ cup of the chilled dressing on each serving.

SOUPS

Noodle 'N' Chicken Soup

This classic soup recipe will make you feel great.

Preparation: 10 minutes

Cooking time: 45 minutes

Ingredients:

1 tbsp unsalted butter

½ small onions, diced

2 carrots, chopped

2 celery stalks, chopped

1 large chicken breast, boneless and skinless, cut into 2-inch squares

1 pinch Italian seasoning

2 cups chicken stock

1 cup water

¼ tsp dried sage

½ tsp salt

¼ tsp ground dry pepper

1 small bay leaf

3 oz egg noodles

Directions:

1. Melt the butter in a pot and sauté the carrots, celery and onions for 5 minutes until tender. Put in the chicken and the Italian seasoning; stir. Allow to cook for 5 minutes until the chicken is almost heated through.

2. Put in the water, chicken stock bay leaf, salt and dried sage; bring to boil and then simmer for about 30 to 40 minutes. Add the noodles when it's 5 minutes to the end of cooking time.

3. Taste and add more seasoning if required. Serve immediately or refrigerate in an airtight container for not more than a week.

Italian Beef And Veggie Soup

Savor the tastes of Italian cuisine in this mouth watering beef and vegetable soup.

Preparation: 10 minutes

Cooking time: 15 minutes

Ingredients:

14.5-oz can diced tomatoes with basil. garlic and oregano

¼ cup dry medium shell whole grain pasta, uncooked

¾ cup frozen Italian vegetable blend

6 oz lean ground beef

1 tbsp balsamic vinegar

1¾ cups water

2 tsp dry chicken bouillon

¼ tsp garlic powder

Directions:

1. Cook the beef over medium-high heat in a saucepan, stirring often until it's no longer pink and becomes crumbled, about 6 minutes; drain off liquid.

2. Put in the remaining ingredients and turn down heat to medium; simmer until the pasta is soft, about 10 minutes.

Tips: You can replace frozen Italian vegetables with a vegetable blend of cauliflower, squash and green beans. If you want to go vegan, use ½ cup cannellini beans, drained and rinsed, instead of ground beef.

Garlic Mushroom Soup

Experience the creamy garlic taste of this homemade mushroom soup. Yummy...!

Preparation: 10 minutes

Cooking time: 25 minutes

Ingredients:

3 garlic cloves, finely chopped

2 cups fresh mushrooms (white or brown button, crimini or any mix), cleaned and finely chopped

1 tbsp flour dissolved in 1 tbsp water

1 tbsp olive oil

1 tbsp butter

1 bay leaf

1 tsp dried thyme

1 tsp Worcestershire sauce

1 cup chicken stock

1 dash nutmeg

½ cup milk

½ cup heavy cream

Fresh ground black pepper

Kosher salt

To garnish: fresh thyme or parsley

Directions:

1. Heat butter and olive oil in a saucepan over medium heat; add the garlic and sauté lightly. Add the thyme, mushroom, Worcestershire sauce and bay leaf; cook until the mushrooms become dry, about 5 minutes.

2. Pour in the chicken broth, stir and bring to a boil. Turn down the heat and allow to simmer for about 10 minutes. Put in the flour paste and cook, stirring often until it becomes thick.

3. Add nutmeg, pepper and salt to taste. Add the cream and milk; cook until it just begins to simmer. Pour into serving bowls and garnish with the fresh thyme or parsley.

Chicken 'N' Macaroni Vegetable Soup

A colorful and flavorful blend of vegetable, chicken and macaroni.

Preparation: 5 minutes

Cooking time: 25 minutes

Ingredients:

½ cup chopped carrot

½ cup chopped onion

½ cup kidney beans, rinsed and drained

½ cup cauliflower

1 cup shredded fresh spinach

1 tbsp butter

2/3 cup cooked and cubed chicken

14½ ounces chicken broth

1/8 tsp pepper

Seasoned salad croutons (optional)

Directions:

1. Melt the butter in a saucepan and sauté the carrot and onion for 4 minutes until soft and crisp. Add the chicken. broth, macaroni, cauliflower and beans; stir and cook until it starts to boil.

2. Turn down heat and simmer covered, for about 15 to 20 minutes until the vegetables and macaroni are soft. Put in the pepper and spinach and then cook, stirring often until the spinach become wilted.

3. Serve and top with croutons, if preferred. Enjoy!

Creamy Onion Soup

Creamy, delicious, tasty and appetizing.

Preparation: 10 minutes

Cooking time: 60 minutes

Ingredients:

2 large yellow onions. cut into two and sliced thinly

2 tsp Worcestershire sauce

2 tbsp unsalted butter

2 tsp balsamic vinegar

2 baguette slices, toasted

2 tbsp white wine

4 cups beef broth

4 slices Swiss cheese

½ tsp brown sugar

½ tsp salt

½ tsp dried thyme leaves

¼ cup shredded parmesan cheese, divided

1 bay leaf

Ground black pepper to taste

Salt to taste

Directions:

1. Put the butter in a big pot and place over medium heat to melt. Add the onions, sugar and salt; cook and stir constantly for 35 minutes until the onions become caramelized.

2. Add the Worcestershire sauce, white wine, beef broth, bay leaf and thyme to the caramelized onions and simmer for 20 minutes; stir often. Take out the bay leaf and throw away. Add the vinegar, salt and pepper to taste.

3. Pour the soup into two oven-safe bowls and place on a baking sheet. Add the bread, Swiss cheese and parmesan evenly on each bowl of soup. Broil until it bubbles; serve while hot.

Broccoli Green Soup

Get this delicious soup on your table in less than 30 minutes. Great for vegetarians.

Preparation: 10 minutes

Cooking time: 15 minutes

Ingredients:

7 ounces broccoli florets

1 cup (or more if needed) vegetable broth

1 garlic clove, chopped

1 tbsp olive oil

Freshly ground black pepper

Salt

To serve: cream

Directions:

1. In a medium saucepan, heat the oil and sauté the garlic for 1 to 2 minutes. Add the broth and the broccoli and bring to boil.

2. Turn down the heat and allow to simmer until the broccoli becomes soft, about 10 to 12 minutes. Add the pepper and salt to taste and then pour into a blender; process until smooth.

3. Scoop into two serving bowls and then drizzle some cream on top. Serve.

Simple Red Lentil Soup

Preparation: 10 minutes

Cooking time: 25 minutes

Ingredients:

½ tbsp olive oil

½ large carrot, diced

½ yellow onion, diced

½ cup red lentil

1 large celery rib

1/8 tsp salt + more to taste

2 cups low sodium broth or water

1 tbsp lemon juice

1 small bay leaf

To serve: yogurt, olive oil or other toppings

Directions:

1. Pour the olive oil into a Dutch oven or medium saucepan and heat over medium heat. Put in the celery, carrot, 1/8 tsp salt and onion; stir, cover and sauté for 5 minutes until the onion is translucent and soft.

2. Put in the broth or water, bay leaf and lentils; reduce the heat immediately it starts to boil. cover and allow to simmer for about 15 minutes until the lentils starts to disintegrate.

3. Remove from heat and then add the lemon juice and more salt as required. Spoon the soup into serving bowls and serve with olive oil or yogurt. If not eaten immediately, the soup can be preserved in a fridge for up to five days.

Hot 'N' Spicy Soup

Try this hot pepper soup during winter.

Preparation: 10 minutes

Cooking time: 25 minutes

Ingredients:

4 tbsp finely chopped onion

1 bacon strip

2 garlic cloves, minced

1 sweet red pepper, chopped

1 tbsp tomato paste

4 drops hot pepper sauce

1/8 tsp paprika

1 dash cayenne pepper

1 tbsp butter

1 cup chicken broth, divided

1 tbsp flour

¼ tsp salt

½ cup heavy whipping cream

To garnish: more chopped red pepper and chives (optional)

Directions:

1. Cook the bacon in a skillet until crisp; drain on paper towel.

2. Add the garlic, red pepper and onions to the fat left in the skillet and sauté for 4 minutes until the onion is soft. Add the paprika, tomato paste, cayenne pepper and hot pepper sauce; stir until well mixed.

3. Put in ¼ cup of the chicken broth and turn down the heat to simmer for about 5 minutes; leave uncovered. turn off heat and allow to cool for about 10 minutes. Transfer to a blender and puree; keep aside.

4. Put the butter into a saucepan and melt over low heat. Add the flour and keep stirring for 2 minutes until it becomes thick. Add the remaining chicken broth gradually while stirring; increase the heat to medium and bring to boil. Allow to cook for 2 minutes over low heat, stirring regularly.

5. Add the salt and cream gradually; stir. Put in the puree and heat through. Break up the bacon and sprinkle over it. Garnish with chopped red pepper and chives, if desired. Serve.

Pureed Vegetable Soup

You can prepare a tasty homemade vegetable soup in a few minutes following these easy steps.

Preparation: 10 minutes

Cooking time: 8 minutes

Ingredients:

1 tsp vegetable oil

½ onion, chopped

1 garlic clove

2 cups frozen vegetable mix (e.g. cauliflower and broccoli)

1½ cup broth

1 tbsp 2% Greek yogurt

To serve: croutons or crackers (optional)

Directions:

1. Heat the oil over medium heat in a saucepan; sauté the garlic and onion for 3 minutes until soft.

2. Add the broth and the vegetables and cook for 4 - 5 minutes until the vegetables become soft.

3. Remove from heat and puree in a blender until smooth. Pour into two serving bowls and ½ tbsp yogurt to each serving. Top with small crackers or croutons, if preferred. Enjoy!

Easy Corn Soup

Summer time is not complete without this savory corn soup.

Preparation: 10 minutes

Cooking time: 0 minute

Ingredients:

3 cups fresh corn kernels, divided

1 cup chicken broth

½ tbsp finely chopped shallot

3 tbsp finely chopped sweet red pepper

½ tbsp olive oil

¼ tsp thyme leaves

1 dash salt

Corn chips (optional)

Directions:

1. Puree 2½ cups of corn, the shallot and broth in batches until smooth. Pour through a strainer and press down to extract the liquid from solids. Add the salt.

2. To make the topping: mix the remaining ½ cup of corn, olive oil, thyme and red pepper together. Pour the soup into two bowls; spoon the topping on each serving and garnish with corn chip, if preferred.

DESSERTS AND DRINKS

Lemony Cake

Preparation time: 10 minutes

Cooking time: 20 minutes

Ingredients:

4 tbsp sugar

3/8 cup all purpose flour

1/8 tsp baking soda

¼ tsp baking powder

1 pinch of salt

1 tbsp + 2 tsp olive oil

3 tbsp sour cream

1 tbsp fresh lemon juice

Zest of 1 lemon

Yolk of 1 large egg

For the frosting:

8 tbsp powdered sugar

1-2 tsp fresh lemon juice

Directions:

1. Heat your oven to 350°F.

2. Place two well greased ramekins (about 6 oz. each) on a small baking sheet.

3. Mix the flour, sugar, salt, baking powder and soda together in a bowl; keep aside.

4. Combine the sour cream, egg yolk, oil, lemon juice and zest in another bowl; whisk well.

5. Pour half of the dry ingredients into the egg-sour cream mixture and mix thoroughly. Add the other half and mix until well combined.

6. Pour the batter into the ramekins and bake in the hot oven for 20 minutes. It is ready when a toothpick comes out clean after it's inserted into it. Remove from oven and leave to cool.

7. To make the frosting; combine the powdered sugar and 1-2 teaspoons of lemon juice (add more lemon juice if you want the frosting thinner).

Rum Raspberry Jam Cocktail

Preparation: 5 minutes

Cooking time: 0 minute

Ingredients:

¼ cup raspberry jam

4 shots of white rum

Juice of 1 lemon

For garnish: fresh berries

Directions:

1. In a 16-oz. mason jar, mix the lemon juice, raspberry jam and rum. Shake the Mason jar well until the jam completely dissolves.

2. Strain the mixture over ice; garnish with the berries and serve.

Grilled Peach Sundae

This can be made also with grilled pineapples.

Preparation: 15 minutes

Cooking time: 10 minutes

Ingredients:

2 scoops frozen vanilla yogurt or fruit sorbet

2 peaches, halved, pitted

1 tbsp toasted unsweetened roasted coconut

1 tsp olive oil

Directions:

1. Heat up grill to high.

2. Brush oil on the peach halves to coat and then grill until soft.

3. Place the two roasted peach halves in separate bowls; add a scoop of the frozen yogurt/sorbet and the coconut on top. Serve.

Gin Blackberry Jam Cocktail

Preparation: 5 minutes

Cooking time: 0 minute

Ingredients:

¼ cup blackberry jam

4 shots of gin

Juice of 1 lemon

For garnish: fresh blackberries

Directions:

1. Pour the rum, lemon juice and blackberry jam into a 16-oz. mason jar. Shake the Mason jar well until the jam completely dissolves.

2. Strain the mixture over ice; garnish with the blackberries and serve.

Crispy Rhubarb Ramekins
A fast and easy dessert recipe that can be prepared at anytime.

Preparation time: 15 minutes

Cooking time: 30 minutes

Ingredients:

1 cup thinly cut rhubarb

3 tbsp granulated sugar

½ cup peeled and chopped apple

¼ tsp + 1/8 tsp ground cinnamon, separated

1 tsp instant tapioca

2 tbsp old fashioned rolled oats

2 tbsp all-purpose flour

3 tsp finely chopped pecan

1½ tbsp dark brown sugar

2 tsp maple syrup

1 tbsp unsalted butter, melted

1/8 tsp salt

Directions:

1. Preheat your oven to 350°F.

2. In a bowl, mix the rhubarb, tapioca, granulated sugar, ¼ tsp cinnamon and apple together. Share the mixture between two custard cups or ramekins of 10-oz each.

3. In another bowl, combine the butter, oats, flour, brown sugar, pecan, salt and 1/8 tsp cinnamon until it feels crumbly. Sprinkle the mixture over the rhubarb-apple mixture in the ramekins.

4. Place in hot oven and bake for 30 minutes until it's slightly brown and bubbling. Leave to cool for about 5 minutes; serve.

Tips: Use rhubarb with red and firm stalks for this recipe. cut them into very thin slices so you won't need to peel the outer strings.

Roasted Berry Peaches

Preparation time: 10 minutes

Cooking time: 20 minutes

Ingredients:

½ cup fresh blueberries

2 ripe peaches, cut into halves and pitted

2 tsp lemon juice

3 tsp brown sugar

4 tsp butter

Directions:

1. Set the 2 peach halves on two 12-inch sq. heavy duty foil cut side facing upwards. Sprinkle each peach half with the sugar, lemon juice and berries; dab with the butter. Wrap both foils over the peaches and close tightly.

2. Place on grill over medium-low heat and cover. Cook for 18 to 20 minutes until soft. When done, open the foil gently to let off steam. Serve.

Vodka Apricot Jam Cocktail

Preparation: 5 minutes

Cooking time: 0 minute

Ingredients:

¼ cup apricot jam

4 shots of vodka

Juice of 1 lemon

For garnish: lemon, mint

Directions:

1. In a mason jar, combine all the ingredients except the garnish and shake the jar thoroughly until the jam dissolves completely.

2. Strain the mixture and add some ice. Garnish with the mint and lemon; serve.

Streusel Pumpkin Custard

This tasty blend of spiced custard and streusel is great for cold weather.

Preparation: 10 minutes

Cooking time: 35 minutes

Ingredients:

4 tbsp brown sugar

1 egg

¼ tsp ground cinnamon

¼ tsp salt

¼ tsp vanilla extract

1/8 tsp ground ginger

1/8 tsp allspice

1/8 tsp nutmeg

½ cup evaporated milk

2/3 cup canned pumpkin

 For the topping:

2 tsp all-purpose flour

3 tsp brown sugar

¼ tsp ground cinnamon

2 tbsp finely chopped pecan

1 tsp butter

Directions:

1. Break the egg into a bowl and whisk; put in the salt, vanilla, spices and sugar. Stir to combine and then add the milk and pumpkin; Stir again to mix well.

2. Grease two 8 or 10-ounce custard cups and pour the mixture into them. Place in the oven at 325°F and bake for 20 minutes.

3. In the meantime, mix the sugar, cinnamon and flour for the topping in a bowl. Add the butter and mix until crumbly; put in the pecans and stir.

4. Sprinkle the topping over the custard after the first 20 minutes of baking. Place bake into the oven and bake for another 15 minutes until a knife come out clean when inserted.

Crumbly Cherry Bars

Preparation: 30 minutes

Cooking time: 26 minutes

Ingredients:

3 tbsp unsalted butter, melted + extra for oiling pan

2 tbsp dried cherries, finely diced

2 tbsp cherry preserves

4 tbsp quick-cooking oats

4 tbsp all-purpose flour

2 tsp confectioners' sugar

2 tbsp packed brown sugar

1 pinch salt

1 pinch baking soda

1 tbsp sliced almonds (skin-on)

Directions:

1. Place a small baking sheet in the lowest rack of the oven and then preheat to 375°F.

2. Line a mini loaf pan with parchment paper so that it extends midway up the longer ends; grease the paper slightly with butter at the bottom and heavily on all the sides.

3. Mix the dried cherries and the preserves in a bowl. Combine the oats, flour, salt, baking soda and sugars in another bowl. Drizzle the melted butter into the flour mixture and stir with a fork until it becomes moist and begins to clump.

4. Measure about half cup of the flour mixture (don't press into the cup) and pour into the prepared mini loaf pan and press to the bottom. Scatter the cherry mixture over it.

5. Put almonds into the flour mixture left and squeeze together to make larger chunks. Spread the flour- almond mixture over the cherry mixture in the pan and press in slightly.

6. Place pan on the baking sheet and bake for 24 - 26 minutes or until the streusel become brown and the cherry bubbly.

7. Place on a cooling rack to cool. When warm, pull out the bar using the parchment paper and then remove paper gently. Leave bar on the rack to cool to room temperature; cut diagonally into two. Enjoy!

Creamy Carrot Cake

You don't need to shy away from baking cakes because you want to prevent waste. Try this!

Preparation: 2 hours 22 minutes (includes cooling time)

Cooking time: 33 minutes

Ingredients:

For the cake:

3 small carrots (about 5 oz), finely grated (making 1 cup)

4 tbsp pecans

2/3 cup all-purpose flour

½ cup granulated sugar

½ tsp ground cinnamon

1 tsp baking powder

¼ tsp salt

1 pinch grated nutmeg

1 large size egg

½ tsp vanilla extract

4 tbsp vegetable oil

For the frosting:

8 tbsp unsalted butter, at room temperature

8 oz cream cheese, at room temperature

½ tsp vanilla extract

¾ cup confectioners' sugar

Directions:

1. To make the cake; preheat oven to 350°F and apply cooking spray lightly to a 9x2" parchment paper-lined round cake pan.

2. Place the pecans on a baking tray and toast for 8 minutes until aromatic and slightly brown. Allow to cool and then chop the baked pecans roughly.

3. In a bowl, combine the baking powder, flour, nutmeg, salt and cinnamon. Make a hole in the middle of the mixture so that the base of the bowl is visible. Add the egg and sugar into the hole and whisk thoroughly with a fork until properly mixed.

4. Put in the vanilla extract and oil and whisk to mix. Combine the wet and dry ingredients using a fork; add the toasted pecans and the carrots and then fold in. Pour the batter into the greased pan.

5. Bake for 20 - 25 minutes until a knife inserted comes out clean. Place on a cooling rack to cool for about 20 minutes; remove from pan and leave to cool completely for about an hour.

6. To make the frosting; put the butter and cream cheese into the food processor and process until smooth and well blended. While processing, stop at intervals to scrape the sides and base of the bowl. Put in the vanilla and confectioners' sugar and blend; pour the frosting into a bowl.

7. To arrange; slice the cake into four equal wedges. Use a spatula to apply 3 tbsp of the frosting on top of each wedge. Stack each wedge on the other on a platter to form a 4 layered cake with frosting on top; also frost the curved sides of the wedges. Place in a fridge for about 30 minutes; cut into two and serve.

Orange Creamy-Dream Shake

Shake-up your day with this creamy blend of yogurt and orange sherbet.

Preparation: 2 minutes

Cooking time: 0 minute

Ingredients:

½ cup frozen vanilla yogurt

½ cup orange sherbet

½ tsp vanilla extract

1 cup milk (low fat)

Directions:

1. Pour the yogurt, milk, sherbet and vanilla extract into a blender; process until smooth.

2. Pour into glasses and serve.

Mixed Berry Tortilla Strips

This Mexican dessert will surely delight your taste buds.

Preparation: 5 minutes

Cooking time: 10 minutes

Ingredients:

1 flour tortilla (8 inches), sliced into thin, short strips

1/8 tsp ground cinnamon

¼ cup fresh blueberries

1 cup sliced fresh strawberries

1 tsp honey

Original dairy whipped topping (chilled, in spray can)

Cooking spray

Directions:

1. Preheat an oven to 350°F.

2. Mix the tortilla chips, cinnamon and honey together in a bowl; toss gently to coat. Arrange the strips on a parchment paper-line baking sheet in one layer and apply cooking spray to coat

3. Place into hot oven and bake until the strips are slightly browned, about 8 - 10 minutes. Remove and set aside to cool.

4. Share the berries between two serving plates, add the whipped topping and garnish with the baked tortillas. Serve and enjoy.

Italian Soda Floats

These floats can keep a couple floating in high spirits after a great meal.

Preparation: 5 minutes

Cooking time: 0 minute

Ingredients:

2 cups club soda

2/3 cup raspberry sorbet

2 tbsp half and half

For garnish: mint

Directions:

1. Share the sorbet equally between two highball glasses. Add 1 cup of club soda and 1 tbsp of half and half into each glass.

2. Finish up with a mint garnish and a straw.

Toasted Coconuts In Tapioca

Preparation: 30 minutes

Cooking time: 5 minutes

Ingredients:

4 tsp quick cooking tapioca, uncooked

3 tbsp sugar

¾ cup light coconut milk

¾ cup milk (fat free)

¼ tsp vanilla extract

2 tbsp egg substitute

1 dash of salt

2 tbsp sweetened coconut flakes, toasted

Directions:

1. In a sauce pan, combine the milk, sugar, tapioca, coconut milk, egg substitute and salt; allow to stand for 5 minutes.

2. Place over medium-high heat and bring to boil stirring regularly. Turn off heat, add the vanilla and stir.

3. Share the mixture equally between two serving dishes; cover and place in a fridge to cool. Top with 1 tbsp of coconut flakes per serving.

The End

Printed in Great Britain
by Amazon